Comedy & Comedians

Acting: Stage & Screen

Art Festivals & Galleries:
The Art of Selling Art

Comedy & Comedians

Filmmaking & Documentaries

Music & Musicians

Painting

Performing Arts

Photography

Sculpting

Writing: Stories, Poetry, Song, & Rap

Comedy &
Comedians

Z.B. Hill

Mason Crest
450 Parkway Drive, Suite D
Broomall, PA 19008
www.masoncrest.com

Printed and bound in the United States of America.

First printing
9 8 7 6 5 4 3 2 1

Series ISBN: 978-1-4222-3167-8
ISBN: 978-1-4222-3170-8
ebook ISBN: 978-1-4222-8707-1

Library of Congress Cataloging-in-Publication Data

Hill, Z. B.
  Comedy & comedians / Z.B. Hill.
      pages cm
  Includes bibliographical references and index.
  ISBN 978-1-4222-3170-8 (hardback) — ISBN 978-1-4222-3167-8 (series) — ISBN 978-1-4222-8707-1 (ebook) 1. Comedy. 2. Comedians. I. Title. II. Title: Comedy and comedians.
  PN1922.H54 2014
  792.23—dc23
                                                      2014011827

Contents

KEY ICONS TO LOOK FOR:

Text-Dependent Questions: These questions send the reader back to the text for more careful attention to the evidence presented there.

Words to Understand: These words with their easy-to-understand definitions will increase the reader's understanding of the text, while building vocabulary skills.

Series Glossary of Key Terms: This back-of-the book glossary contains terminology used throughout this series. Words found here increase the reader's ability to read and comprehend higher-level books and articles in this field.

Research Projects: Readers are pointed toward areas of further inquiry connected to each chapter. Suggestions are provided for projects that encourage deeper research and analysis.

Sidebars: This boxed material within the main text allows readers to build knowledge, gain insights, explore possibilities, and broaden their perspectives by weaving together additional information to provide realistic and holistic perspectives.

Words to Understand

improvise: Create and perform without any preparation ahead of time, completely on the spur of the moment off the top of your head.

traditional: Having to do with the way things have always been done.

troupe: A group of performers who tour together.

prestigious: Inspiring respect and admiration; having high status.

Chapter One

Creating Comedy

You may be surprised to learn that comedy is an art. Comedy is a performance that is meant to be funny and to make people laugh. It comes in lots of different forms, from comedic plays to TV shows to stand-up comedian shows. Comedy has offended some people, and it's not an art that everyone enjoys. But it has definitely brought a lot of smiles to people's faces over time!

THE ART OF COMEDY

Comedians don't normally just get up on stage and deliver a bunch of jokes they're thinking up on the spot. They actually take a long time to think about their jokes, and they try them out on people to see if they get good reactions. A comedic performance is usually well thought out

Margaret Cho has many accomplishments, but she's most famous as a stand-up comedian who uses her work to speak out against racism and gay prejudice.

Make Connections: Comedy vs. Humor

 Comedy and humor are not quite the same thing. Humor is anything that makes us laugh. Anybody can practice humor. Any time you crack a joke or say something funny that amuses other people, that's humor. You don't have to be a professional. Comedy, on the other hand, is more structured than humor. Comedy is performed by someone (the comedian). It is a series of humorous jokes or situations that make people laugh but may also make them think more deeply about the subject of the comedy.

and practiced. Some comedians may *improvise*, but most know what they're going to say before they step on stage or in front of the camera.

Art also makes people think more deeply or differently about life. Comedy can definitely do that. A comedian isn't always just telling jokes to make people feel good. She's also telling those jokes to make a point. If she's an Asian American performing comedy about race, like comedian Margaret Cho, she's not just making people laugh. She's pointing out racism in a humorous way that makes it easier for people to think about it.

Comedy has its place with other more *traditional* performing arts. Painting, sculpture, and photography are all visual arts, because they produce an object you can see. Performing arts include dance, music, and acting. Performing artists use their bodies and some tools (such as instruments) to produce art that isn't visible. A dance performance, singing, music, and a play are definitely real, but they don't produce an object like visual art. Comedy is like performing art in that way. A comedian performs on stage or in front of a camera to produce his art in front of other people.

The word "slapstick" started out because early comedians actually used sticks as part of their skits. The sticks were made of two slats, so that when the sticks struck something, they made a big noise as the slats slapped against each other. To the audience, it sounded as though the sticks were doing a lot of damage, when they actually weren't. This nineteenth-century painting shows a harlequin (or clown) holding a "slap stick."

TYPES OF COMEDY

Comedy comes in different forms. You may think one kind of comedy is hilarious, while another one is boring or not very funny at all. Some of the types include:

- Slapstick. Slapstick involves physical humor and often getting hurt. People laugh when someone slips on a skateboard or falls off a ladder. Comedy movies often contain slapstick humor.
- Satire. When a comedic performance makes fun of a big idea or current events, it's satire. A comedian might make fun of politicians, war, or school. Satire does more than make fun of things, though—it also points out things that the comedian thinks should be changed to make the world a better place.
- Irony. An ironic situation is one in which the opposite of what you expect to happen actually happens.
- Sarcasm. A comedian who is sarcastic insults someone or something in order to make fun of the person or an idea. Sarcasm can be mean, but it can also be funny.
- Screwball. Screwball comedy contains situations that would never happen in real life. The actors or comedians involved in the situation respond in ways that usually just make the situation worse.
- Stand-up. A stand-up comedian may use any of these kinds of comedy while performing in front of a live audience. She might have a theme, like race or gender, or she might cover a whole range of things.

Comedians might specialize in one kind of comedy over another. The Three Stooges are the classic example of slapstick comedians, as they bungle their way through situations by poking and punching each other. John Stewart's *The Daily Show* is a good example of satire, since he pretends to seriously deliver the news but is actually making fun of society and the media.

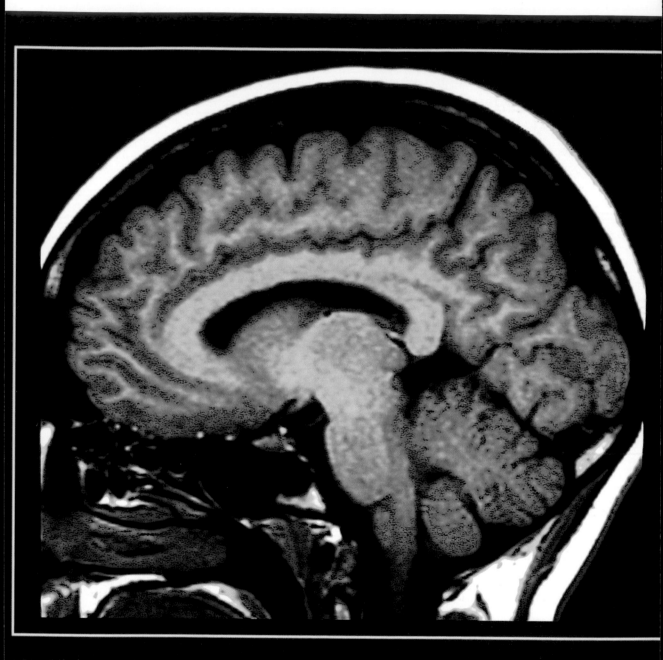

Using modern technology like the MRI scan shown here, researchers can actually see the way laughter changes what's going on inside the human brain.

THE POWER OF HUMOR

Just about everyone can agree that humor and laughing are necessary parts of a good life, even if we can't all agree on what's funny. Laughing feels good and can lift a bad mood.

Even scientists agree that laughter is good for you. Greek doctors, Native American healers, and medieval surgeons have all prescribed humor and laughter for their patients throughout history.

Today, doctors still recognize the health benefits of humor and laughing. Laughter is good for both your mind and your body. When you're stressed out, nervous, or in pain, funny things that make you laugh can distract you and make you feel better. Some psychologists prescribe laughter therapy for depressed patients.

When you laugh or find something funny, something happens in your brain. Your brain sends out a chemical called dopamine, which is one of the chemicals that make you experience positive feelings. If you can increase your dopamine levels, you feel happier.

Researchers also agree that laughing with someone else is even better than laughing alone. When you're laughing with someone, it's hard to be mad at her or feel badly about her. Laughter brings you together with friends, family, and even enemies. When you're feeling better, you can have better relationships with other people.

One doctor in particular promoted laughter as medicine. Dr. Norman Cousins was diagnosed with a serious disease in 1964. He tried regular medicine, but that didn't work, so he looked for alternatives. He ended up taking lots of Vitamin C and also watched a lot of comedy movies. He credited the laughter that came out of watching the movies with helping him sleep and eventually recover from his disease, so that he could live many more years. After that, Dr. Cousins funded studies on laughter therapy, and he wrote books and articles about it.

Around the same time, another doctor was also using the health effects of laughter. Patch Adams is a doctor who founded the Gesundheit! Institute, a hospital that also includes care with humor and compassion.

Tina Fey has proven to the world that women can be just as funny as men. She's considered to be at the top of her field, one of the most talented comedians in the business.

Make Connections: Some Ways to Laugh More

If you're feeling blue or sick, you might want to look for some more ways to laugh. You'll be feeling better before you know it.

- Watch a funny movie or TV show
- Hang out with your funniest friends
- Read a book of jokes or other funny book
- Go to a laughter yoga class or join a laughter club
- Play with little kids
- Play with a pet

Caretakers at the Institute often use clowns to make patients laugh. The doctor's efforts were made into a movie starring Robin Williams in 1998.

FAMOUS COMEDIANS

Right now, comedians are popular. The list of comedians on TV, in the movies, and on stage is pretty long. Near the top is comedian Tina Fey.

Fey is best known for her performances on *Saturday Night Live* and in the show *30 Rock*. She was born in Pennsylvania in 1970, where she had a fairly quiet childhood and then went on to study drama at the University of Virginia. She realized she wanted a career in comedy, so she moved to Chicago, where lots of comedians get their start. Young people who want to make it big in comedy enroll in training classes at Second City, a theater, comedy ***troupe***, and program for budding comedians. Many now-famous comedians have gone through Second City.

Saturday Night Live (SNL) noticed Fey and her skit ideas. The show offered her a position as a writer. She became the show's first female

Research Project

 This chapter gives the backgrounds of two famous and successful comedians. Find another comedian and do some research on him or her. Look online or in your library for information about the comedian's background, type of comedy, and how and where he or she performs. Write a paragraph or two about each of those three topics.

head writer in history after she had worked there for a few years. Then, while still writing, she also became a performer on *SNL*. She's well known now for both her writing and her acting. Besides *SNL* skits, she has also written and acted in the movie *Mean Girls*, written a humorous autobiography, and twice hosted the Golden Globes, among other accomplishments.

Fey also created and starred in the TV show *30 Rock*, about the head writer of a sketch comedy show based in New York. Although the show was fictional, Fey drew on her own experiences as a head writer in a similar situation. The show won three Emmys for Outstanding Comedy Series in 2007, 2008, and 2009. Fey herself won Outstanding Lead Actress in a Comedy Series in 2008.

Though you might not have heard of him yet, Russell Peters is another famous comedian. Peters is a classic stand-up comedian who is extremely popular in Canada, Australia, Asia, and other places around the world.

Peters was born in Ontario in Canada in 1970. He is a mix of British and Indian heritage, which provides a lot of background for his comedy. He started out performing stand-up in Toronto. After videos he uploaded

Text-Dependent Questions

1. Why is comedy considered an art?
2. What is the difference between the visual and performing arts?
3. Name two types of comedy and describe them.
4. According to the sidebar, how is comedy different than humor?
5. How do laughter and humor help you feel better?

to YouTube went viral, people started to pay attention to him. His comedy focuses on racism and the experience of being a person of mixed heritage in North America. He tells humorous stories about his own life, his childhood, and his family

Peters is known for selling out huge performance venues in just a few hours. In 2007, he was the first comedian to sell out the Air Canada Centre in Toronto in just two days. He has also hosted the largest stand-up comedy show ever in Australia and in Singapore. He has sold out shows in New York City, London, Sydney, and more.

Peters' comedy albums called *Outsourced* and *Red, White, and Brown* are just as popular as his live performances. All this success has meant that Forbes magazine has rated him one of the highest-paid comedians. He has also won a Gemini Award, one of the most **prestigious** entertainment awards in Canada.

Comedians like Tina Fey and Russell Peters belong to a long history of comedy. Their modern-day comedy builds on the comedy of the past.

Words to Understand

emcee: Short for "master of ceremonies"; the person who introduces entertainers at a show or event.

controversial: Causing arguments and disagreement.

mainstream: Having to do with the ideas, attitudes, and activities that the majority of a population considers to be "normal."

Chapter Two

The History of Comedy and Comedians

The idea of comedy is pretty old. Probably as soon as there were humans, they were making each other laugh, although we don't have any recorded evidence of this sort of prehistoric humor. We do have lots of evidence for comedy and comedians from the Greek age all the way up to today. That equals a lot of people laughing!

ANCIENT COMEDY

The first time a group of people came up with the concept of comedy was in ancient Greece. The word comedy actually comes from a Greek word: komodios, which means "actor or singer in the revels" (revels were

Actors in ancient Greek comedies often wore masks such as this one.

rowdy festivals). Greek comedy is based on the theater and on acting, both of which happened during festivals.

The Greeks celebrated a festival honoring the god Dionysus, the god of winemaking and fertility. People sang in choirs and put on performances that were a lot like plays. Theaters were built to hold these plays. We call the kind of comedic performances put on by the first ancient Greeks Old Comedy. The first Old Comedy play that researchers have discovered is from about 450 BCE. These performances were very lively and often made fun of people and things.

Comedic plays followed a similar structure in Ancient Greece. First, a chorus of singers performed song and dance while wearing bizarre outfits. For example, in a play called *The Wasps*, the singers wore bee costumes complete with stingers. We would probably find that funny even today! Next, actors came on and had a lively, funny debate. Each actor might play several different characters in multiple different settings. The costume and set changes happened very quickly. The third part of the play allowed the members of the chorus to speak to the audience, which can often still be part of modern-day comedy performances. Finally, the chorus sang more songs and danced more dances as they left. People entered their plays into contests during festivals. A few comedies were chose to be performed during the festival. Judges would vote for their favorites and award the winner.

By a few centuries later, comedic plays were more romantic and intelligent. Historians call this period New Comedy. In this period, Greek comedies had plots that made more sense and focused more on the actors rather than the chorus. Most of them had five acts.

One of the most famous Greek comedic writer was Aristophanes, who lived from about 460 to 380 BCE. He wrote at least eleven plays. They focused on highlighting some of the ways that society was ridiculous, and made fun of many politicians. In his play *The Wasps*, he says:

Oh would some god, with a sudden stroke,
Convert me to a cloud of smoke!

These figures portray three of the standard characters in commedia dell'arte: the harlequin (or clown); a figure named "Pantalone," who represented money and greed; and the doctor.

Like politicians' words I rise
In gaseous vapor to the skies.

COMEDY THROUGH THE AGES

Comedy didn't end in Greece. The Romans adopted it after they became more powerful in Europe than the Greeks. Like a lot of other Greek ideas, the Romans took comedy and spread it around their large empire. They also created some of their own comedy.

A few hundred years later in Italy, comedic performers turned to a style of comedy called commedia dell'arte. The name most closely translates to "comedy of craft." Commedia dell'arte was improvised, so the actors had no written lines. However, there were standard characters. Every commedia dell'arte play could pick from a list of characters that everyone knew. There were greedy merchants, silly old men, and mischievous servants. Audiences could always identify the characters based on their speech, their costumes, and their personalities.

Although commedia dell'arte started in Italy, it traveled all over Europe during the 1600s. Commedia dell'arte was equal parts theater and humor, and influenced later comedy styles.

One of the greatest comedians of all time isn't someone you might think of immediately: William Shakespeare. Many of Shakespeare's plays are extremely funny, even if sometimes the humor gets lost on modern audiences struggling to figure out his language.

Shakespeare lived in England from around 1564 to 1616. We don't know a lot about his life, but we do know he was a poet and playwright. He was born in the country and moved to London probably in the 1590s. He was an actor in an acting group called the King's Men. He also wrote and released many poems and plays. People thought he was a good writer—but it wasn't until later that he became known as perhaps the greatest writers of all time.

Shakespeare's plays are good examples of some of the comedies of a few hundred years ago. Comedy wasn't something that happened on TV or at the movies, or even in books. Comedy happened on stage. Some of Shakespeare's plays were dramas—serious plays with sad endings, but others were comedies, such as *A Midsummer Night's Dream* or *Much Ado About Nothing*. Shakespeare's comedies contain funny scenes and lines, and they end on a positive note, rather than in death like his other, dramatic plays. Shakespeare's comedies are mostly romantic comedies.

Posters like this one let people know that a vaudeville show was coming to town.

Make Connections: Traveling Shows

 Vaudeville is a type of traveling show that was circling around the United States in the nineteen and twentieth centuries. Wild West shows with cowboys and Indians, circuses, and minstrel shows also traveled from town to town putting on performances. In the age before TV, movies, and even radio, people relied on live shows for their entertainment.

Comedy isn't just limited to European countries, though. Plenty of other places in the world have a long tradition of humor and comedy too. In central Asia, a philosopher named Nasreddin Hoja lived many hundreds of years ago, in what is now Azerbaijan. Humorous stories about him have been told for a long time. Many of them have to do with Hoja and the powerful king Timur (also called Tamerlane). One story says that Timur was unhappy with a tax collector and ordered him to eat his tax books, which he then did. Then Timur appointed Hoja as the replacement tax collector. The king wanted to see how his new tax collector was performing, so he sent for him. Hoja entered the court to show him his records to prove he was doing a good job. All of his tax records were written on flat bread! Timur was immediately angry, but Hoja replied, "Your Highness, these are the tax books. I might have to eat them."

STAND-UP

Stand-up comedy is much different from the old comedic plays. Stand-up comedy is also much newer than earlier forms of comedy. It grew in the United States in the 1800s. Some people say its roots stretch back to lecturers who traveled and told funny stories, like Mark Twain.

The Three Stooges' slapstick humor started out as vaudeville routines, but they ended up in films and television shows that are still shown on TV today. More than fifty years later, they are still making people laugh.

In the early twentieth century, vaudeville was popular. Vaudeville was a traveling show of performers of all sorts—dancers, singers, magicians, contortionists, musicians, actors, and lecturers. It didn't have a story or a plotline like with plays. Each performer did his or her own segment, independent of all the others. Some performers entertained the audience with some memorized short humorous routines. Each show usually had a master of ceremonies who sometimes improvised jokes.

Make Connections: Who's On First?

One of the most famous early stand-up routines features Bud Abbott and Lou Costello. These two comedians were vaude-ville stars who transitioned into radio, film, and TV. They per-formed a well-know skit about baseball players named Who, What, and I Don't Know. Here's only a short part of their act:

Costello: Look Abbott, if you're the coach, you must know all the players.

Abbott: I certainly do.

Costello: Well you know I've never met the guys. So you'll have to tell me their names, and then I'll know who's playing on the team...

Abbott: Well, let's see, we have on the bags, Who's on first, What's on sec-ond, I Don't Know is on third...

Costello: That's what I want to find out.

Abbott: I say Who's on first, What's on second, I Don't Know's on third.

Costello: Are you the manager?

Abbott: Yes.

Costello: You gonna be the coach too?

Abbott: Yes.

Costello: And you don't know the fellows' names?

Abbott: Well I should.

Costello: Well then who's on first?

Abbott: Yes.

Costello: I mean the fellow's name.

Abbott: Who.

Costello: The guy on first.

Abbott: Who.

Costello: The first baseman.

Abbott: Who.

Costello: The guy playing...

Abbott: Who is on first!

Johnny Carson chats on *The Tonight Show* with Ronald Reagan in 1975, when Reagan was governor of California. Carson's comedy style influenced other comedians and comedy shows that came after him.

One of the first stand-up comedians was Bob Hope. Hope was born in England and started out as a vaudeville performer and ***emcee***. Later on he hosted his own radio program that included jokes and humor, and he traveled around entertain military troops with his comedy routines. Hope did a lot to move comedy from vaudeville to real stand-up.

An important area where comedy was growing was called the

Make Connections: British Stand-up

 Although stand-up comedy started out in the United States, it also traveled around the world. In Great Britain, comedians with a slightly different take on comedy took the stage. The comedy group Monty Python was popular, and so were individual comedians especially in the north of England.

Borscht Belt. In the early and mid-twentieth century, Jews from New York City went north during the summer to resorts in the Catskill Mountains. The area was called the Borscht Belt, after the beet soup made by many Jewish immigrants.

The resorts put on shows for their guests, and many of them were comedy shows. Lots of the early stand-up comedians started out in the Borscht Belt and shared similar comedic styles. In the resorts, comedians used classic jokes less and less. Instead, they created the humorous dialogue we're used to today. Rodney Dangerfield, Phyllis Diller, Sid Caesar, Mel Brooks, and Lenny Bruce are all examples of comedians who got their start or were influenced by the Borscht Belt.

Comedians kept reforming their techniques and shows through the next few decades. They left vaudeville behind as films and TV took over. And over time, comedy became more **controversial** and less good-natured. It became more critical of the way things were in the United States, especially politics. Some comedians, like Lenny Bruce, got in trouble with the law for their outspoken opinions.

George Carlin became one of the most famous comedians of this time. Carlin was the comedian that represented the change and the unrest that was going on in the 1960s. He made fun of traditional values,

Mel Brooks, who would later become famous as a creator of funny movies, got his start as a stand-up comedian on the Borscht Belt.

Research Project

Comedy has been very popular in the United States, but other countries have also seen comedy and comedians soar in popularity. Search online to see where comedy is popular in other parts of the world. Pick a country and do some more research to find out the history of comedy in that country, what the humor is like, and who some of the most famous comedians in that country are.

the Vietnam War, politics, and the middle class. Carlin and other comedians helped people see what was wrong with society using humor.

Richard Pryor was another comedian of this kind. Pryor, who was African American, highlighted race and ghetto culture. He told stories about his experiences as a black American, and was able to tell the truth about those experiences through making people laugh.

In the 1970s, comedians started on a new theme. Many comedians made comedy personal. They made jokes about their lives and the other people in their lives. Comedy was an observation about daily life, something that comedians still do today. This style of comedy is called observational stand-up.

Comedians were also becoming even more **mainstream**. Steve Martin sold out huge arenas that seated 20,000 people and lots more people were buying his albums full of comedy routines. Martin was just the first of the hugely popular comedians to come along. Clubs devoted to stand-up comedy popped up, and not just in big cities like New York.

COMEDY ON TV AND IN THE MOVIES

Comedians performed a lot on stage, especially in New York City. But there were also comedians on TV. *The Tonight Show* was the most popular comedy show on TV. Johnny Carson hosted the show for thirty years, followed by Jay Leno, Conan O'Brien, and Jimmy Fallon. The host performs humorous segments and invites celebrities for interviews. *The Tonight Show* has been on TV since 1954 and is still on the air. Other late night comedy shows joined it, like *The Night Show*, *Saturday Night Live (SNL)*, and *The Late Late Show*.

By the 1980s and 1990s, comedy expanded beyond talk and skit shows to sitcoms. *Seinfeld* was comedian Jerry Seinfeld's TV show about a bunch of single people living their lives in New York City. Bill Cosby's *The Cosby Show* told the story of an African-American family. Roseanne Barr acted in *Roseanne*, about a working-class family in the Midwest. All these shows starred the comedians as the leads. By the twenty-first century, other TV sitcoms featured actors who got their start in comedy. *30 Rock* starred Tina Fey, a former *Saturday Night Live* performer. *Parks and Recreation* starred Amy Poehler, who also performed on *SNL* and comedian Aziz Ansari. Stand-up comedian Louis C.K. had his own show simply called *Louie*.

Today, comedy, news, and politics mix quite a bit on TV. *The Daily Show* with Jon Stewart and *The Colbert Report* with Steven Colbert make fun of current news by pretending to be news anchors.

Comedy is also a familiar film genre. Comedy films make people laugh. Like other forms of comedy (on stage, for example), film comedy comes in different varieties. Slapstick comedy has been popular since the beginning of comedic film. Early slapstick stars include the Three Stooges and Charlie Chaplin. More modern slapstick comedy films include *Home Alone*, National Lampoon movies, and *The Jerk* with Steve Martin. Of course, plenty of comedy films aren't slapstick; there are romantic comedies, black comedies (where humor makes light of serious situations), screwball comedies, and more.

Some stand-up or TV comedians make the move into film. *Saturday Night Live* is especially well known for being the beginning place for many comedy stars in the movies. The list is long, but some of them

Text-Dependent Questions

1. Who were the first group of people to develop the idea of comedy? Were they likely the first people to ever find something funny?
2. What sort of performance did comedy start out as?
3. Why is Shakespeare considered a comedy writer?
4. What was vaudeville, and how did it influence stand-up comedy?
5. What are two TV shows that star stand-up comedians as the central actors?

include Tina Fey, Will Farrell, Eddie Murphy, Bill Murray, Adam Sandler, Chevy Chase, Kristin Wiig, and Chris Rock. Many comedy movies feature actors who got their start in stand-up comedy and made the transition to film. These comedians, like the centuries of comedians who had come before them, proved that they were not only artists; they also had what it takes to be successful in the business of comedy.

Words to Understand

routine: A set piece of entertainment that is performed pretty much the same way each time.

refine: To make better; to improve by making small changes to something.

Chapter Three

The Business of Comedy

Comedy may be an art, but it's also a business. For comedians, comedy is a job. They have to go about it in a businesslike way if they hope to succeed.

THE COMEDIANS

Comedians treat their jobs seriously, so that they can find work, get paid, and become better known. A comedian who doesn't treat his work seriously probably won't get very far.

Stand-up comedians who are starting their careers perform at comedy clubs, colleges, large parties and events, and anywhere else they can get a job. They may also try jokes out on their friends and family and practice being funny when they're not on stage.

Making people laugh is a fun job—but if you're just starting out like this stand-up comedian, it can also be a challenging job.

Comedians' schedules can be hectic. Most comedy shows are in the evening or at night, so that's when comedians have to work. Comedians who are just starting out are mostly happy to get any work they can get, so they may end up working every night for a few weeks, if they can get enough gigs. Most comedians have to work on weekends too. While the rest of us want to be entertained on the weekends by going to things like comedy shows, the people performing and those backstage are working!

Comedians also travel a lot. They travel to gigs around the country and sometimes around the world, if they become well known. Comedians who are just starting out want to get as much exposure as possible, so they work as many gigs as they can. They might have to drive hours every week to get from one show to the next. Even big-name comedians have to travel a lot, especially if they're giving world tours and traveling for TV or movie filming.

Make Connections:
Are Comedians Funny People?

 You might think that all comedians are hilarious off stage, in front of their family and friends. That's true for some comedians, but not all. Comedians are also businesspeople, and they take their jobs very seriously. Some comedians are depressed or not naturally funny people, but they enjoy doing comedy as a career. It might even help them deal with the negative things going on in their lives. So if you aren't considered the class clown in your school, it's okay—you can still be a great comedian. On the other hand, even people who are very funny might not make good comedians, if they can't perform on stage or if they don't have any business skills.

Comedians have to work hard to get to the top of their business. Only the most talented ones with the most dedication make it to the headliner stage.

Comedy clubs can be small and not very fancy—or large and sophisticated like this one.

Stand-up comedians usually start out as openers at comedy clubs. Openers get about ten or fifteen minutes to perform a **routine** on stage, and then they introduce the main acts that come after. Openers aren't usually paid very much, but they get their names out there and start to get a fan base.

Once an opener starts to become successful, she might get invited back to a comedy club as a feature act. Feature acts have more time on stage. They are more experienced, but they haven't made it to the top yet. At the top are headliners. They are the reasons people come to the comedy shows in the first place. Headliners have an hour or more

The sound system is an important part of comedy clubs, especially big ones, where the comedian's voice needs to reach to the last row of seats.

to perform on stage. Some comedians might never reach the headliner stage, but the ones who do are considered successful.

COMEDY VENUES

There's another side to the comedy business too. If everyone involved in comedy just performed, there wouldn't be anywhere to perform it! Comedy venues are important parts of the comedy world.

Many clubs around the world are dedicated only to comedy. Other venues might host all sorts of performances, including music and theater, not just comedy. Some comedy venues are tiny, with small stages and a few seats. Some are giant auditoriums also used for huge concerts and sports games. Big or small, comedy venues provide a space for comedians to share their jokes and skits with a big audience.

Comedy venues need a stage, a sound system, and a lighting system. The audience has to be able to hear and see the comedian. Some comedy clubs also have a kitchen so they can serve audience members food and drink.

Some comedy venues have open-mic nights. They don't schedule specific comedians to come and perform. Instead, they invite anyone who wants to come up to the stage to try out their comedy routines. This is how lots of young comedians get their starts. Open-mic nights give them the chance to *refine* their routines and figure out what works and what doesn't. Open-mic nights can be good for comedy venues, because they don't have to pay the performers so they can save money. However, the quality of open-mic performers is hit or miss, so the venue might not be able to attract enough people who want to hear really good comedy.

Comedy clubs range from the tiny to the well known. Many cities or even large towns have a small comedy club that books local talent. Larger cities have bigger comedy clubs that get big-name talent. Chicago, Los Angeles, and New York City are particularly known for their great comedy clubs.

Research Project

Look in the yellow pages or online to find the name of a comedy club somewhere near you. Then see if you can find its schedule of shows. Does the club follow the format of opener, feature, and headliner outlined in this chapter? Do the shows vary based on the day of the week? Do some more research on the club to familiarize yourself with how it works. Then research another comedy club and compare the two.

BEHIND THE SCENES

Besides being on stage, comedians might also work as writers, creating the lines and the scenes the comedic actors perform. Together, performers and writers make some of the best comedy out there.

Becoming a comedy writer is every bit as difficult as becoming a comedy performer. Comedy writers create lines for movies, sketch shows, sitcoms, and even sometimes for stand-up comedians. Stand-up comedians are almost always writers too. They have to come up with their own jokes and routines most of the time, as well as perform them. If they're not good comedy writers, then they won't give very good performances because the most basic layer of their comedy routine won't be very good.

WORKING ON THE SIDE

Most comedians don't start out with full-time comedy jobs. At least at first, they often have to work other jobs in order to make a living. Only

Text-Dependent Questions

1. When do comedians usually have to work during the week?
2. What is an opener?
3. How might an open mic night help a beginning comedian?
4. Why is good writing important for comedy?
5. What kinds of jobs might comedians take when they're not performing or writing?

the most successful comedians can rely on their comedy for enough money to live comfortably.

Some comedians get jobs that have nothing to do with comedy. Maybe they have other interests they want to pursue. Or they want a flexible job like waiting tables, which they can do while they write and perform comedy.

Some comedians find jobs that are in their field, even if it's not actually performing comedy. They might get a job at a comedy club selling tickets or working in the kitchen. It's not exactly what they want to be doing, but it's a step in the right direction. They might also get jobs as writers, advertisers, actors, or journalists.

All of them are willing to do whatever it takes to be in the comedy business. Many of them started out when they were still young. Maybe you can too!

Words to Understand

transcripts: The written version of something that was first presented in another way.

internship: A way to get on-the-job training; you learn while you actually work alongside people who are already established in a particular career. Some internships are paid, but many are not.

Chapter Four

How Can I Get Involved in Comedy?

If you're interested in becoming a comedian or working in the comedy business, you have some work in front of you. You need to have more than some good jokes and a sense of humor. You also need to work hard, practice a lot, and meet the right people. Many people who want to be comedians never make it. But if you stay dedicated to your goals, you just might succeed!

BE AN AUDIENCE MEMBER

As you're just starting out, and even when you become more experienced, see as much comedy as you can. The more you watch, the more

Comedian Steve Martin started his career when he was a teenager. He got a job at Disneyland, where he developed his talent for making people laugh by making balloon animals and juggling. After that, he teamed up with a classmate to do a musical comedy routine at local coffee houses.

you'll understand what's out there. Watching other comedians perform will help you figure out what your own style is. Don't copy other comedians but learn from them. Look for people whose work you admire and can take inspiration from.

Check out comedians who are visiting your area. Going to comedy clubs will show you all levels of comedians. You'll probably see comedians who are just starting out, comedians who have been around and performing for a few years, and much more experienced comedians who have great routines.

Go to comedy movies. Watch TV shows that have comedians. Find YouTube clips online. Rent or buy comedy albums and DVDs. Read some scripts of comedy film or TV to see what comedy writers produce. Reading a script is often very different from watching the final product on screen.

START PERFORMING

You'll never become a comedian if you don't start performing. You need to know how to tell jokes in front of an audience, which only comes with practice. Not only do you need to memorize the jokes, you have to figure out what you're doing with your body on stage while you're talking, decide on the timing of your jokes, and more. No one will laugh at your routine if you sound timid on stage or if you forget the punch line to a joke.

You'll have to do some work behind the scenes too, besides just performing. You have to come up with jokes and stories that people think are funny. Even if you can make people laugh in everyday life, that's not the same as getting up on a stage and keeping people entertained for a while. All eyes are on you, and they're expecting a lot!

Take notes as you think of funny things. Keep a pen and paper or your phone or computer handy so you can write down things as you

Chris Rock is another comedian who got started when he was still a teenager. He was so determined to be a comedian that, as a young adolescent, he showed up at every open mic he could find in New York City. Soon he started getting jobs. By the time he was eighteen, he was an experienced comedian—and ready to be discovered by Eddie Murphy.

Make Connections: Online Classes

 There are lots of online comedy classes out there. Do some research to find out what the most reputable ones are, because some may just take your money and not give you much in return. Online classes are great if you're still in school, if you don't live near a comedy scene, or if you travel a lot.

think of them. Don't think about what you write down—just write. After you take a lot of notes, you might come up with one or two great jokes that you can then practice and perform.

Once you're ready with a few minutes of comedy routine, practice by yourself. If you're comfortable with it, you might decide to start practicing in front of friends or family. Record or film yourself so you can listen later and see what needs improvement and what you've already achieved. You can keep it pretty short at first. Five minutes of comedy is fine when you're starting out. Then you can work your way toward longer routines.

TAKE CLASSES

Like other forms of art, you can take classes to get better at comedy. Instead of painting a vase of flowers or learning dance moves, you'll be learning how to tell jokes and get people laughing.

You probably won't find a comedy class at your school, but there are other places to look. If you happen to live in a large town or city that has a comedy club, see if they ever offer classes. Local community

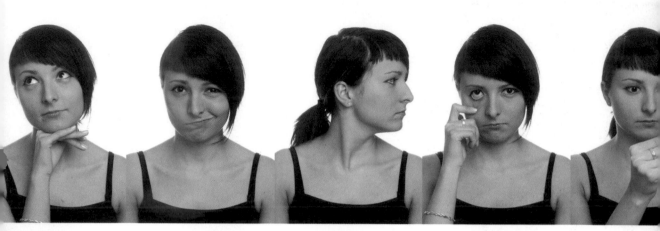

Facial expressions are a part of any successful comedy routine's delivery. Along with good jokes, you'll need to make your face, your voice, and your body work together to make people laugh.

Taking classes to learn more about improv and comedy can be a great way to move forward in your comedy career.

education centers also may offer classes in comedy. Summer camps may be another option for you—a drama, theater or art camp might have a special session or track for comedy.

One thing you won't need to qualify for being a comedian is a college degree in comedy. Currently, Columbia College in Chicago is the only school to offer a bachelor's degree in Comedy. Students can major in theater and concentrate in comedy writing and performance.

Comedian Louis C.K. writes, directs, and stars in his own TV show, *Louie*, proving that succeeding in comedy means more than just being funny.

Make Connections: Advice from the Experts

 Other comedians, comedy writers, and even comedy fans might have some advice for you. For example, here are some tips from a list of fifty featured on the website connectedcomedy.com:

- Be professional.
- Embrace, empower, and appreciate every one of your fans.
- Be patient.
- Don't be afraid to fail.
- Learn the business of comedy.
- Recognize it's not enough to just be funny.
- Don't get jealous of other comedians' success.
- Practice multiple forms of comedy—stand-up, acting, sketch, improv, writing, podcasting.
- Understand what your strengths are as a performer and seek out opportunities to exploit them.

However, a college degree in drama, English, or business might help you on your path to becoming a comedian. You learn a lot in college, not just how to get a specific job. Familiarizing yourself with acting, writing, and the business world will all be very helpful later on. And college campuses are great places to try out comedy routines.

WORK ON YOUR WRITING

All comedians should be good comedic writers. Even if you don't think you'll go into comedy writing as a career, you should be on top of your comedy writing. Plus, it's always good to have a backup plan. If you

Comedian Stephen Colbert got his start when he was working in the box office of Second City, a comedy enterprise in Chicago. He discovered that employees could take classes for free at the training center at Second City, so he signed up—and he eventually built a successful career in comedy.

aren't finding success as a performer, you might want to look into comedy writing instead.

Just like with performing, practice your writing. Write down lots of jokes and have your friends read them. Read **transcripts** of other comedians' routines and see what makes them so funny. Separating the writing from the performance can be a good thing to do, because you won't get distracted by how the comedian is delivering his jokes. You'll just be focused on the writing.

Even if your city or town doesn't offer comedy classes anywhere close by, you can still take writing classes. You'll definitely have to write in school a lot. Instead of complaining about writing essays and test answers, use the time to really polish your writing skills. If you have to write short story or a poem, write something funny. If you can make someone laugh, and it's well written, you're on your way to becoming a better comedy writer.

When it's time, try and find a job or an **internship** at a TV or movie production company. That way, you'll know more how the production business works, and who you might want to talk to about becoming a writer. For example, being a writer's assistant would be a great way to move up to the next step. You should also always have some samples of your writing handy, in case you have the chance to pass it along to someone who might be able to give you a job if she thinks your work is good.

NETWORK

Almost no one becomes successful on her own. It's all about the people you know in the comedy world (and for most careers). Knowing the right people will help you move up in comedy. If you never speak to anyone, or if you're unpleasant and unfriendly, you'll have a much harder time becoming successful. Networking is the term that refers to meeting new

Research Project

Check out some comedians' websites to see if they post their backgrounds. Look at both famous and beginning comedians. How did they get their start in comedy? How did they get ahead? Write down anything you find helpful. You should also write down any advice they have for beginners like you.

people and connecting with them about opportunities in your chosen profession. Networking can help you out a lot in comedy.

Start off with your local comedy scene. Talk to the people who work in comedy clubs, or even the manager. E-mail comedy clubs if you don't live close to one. Even if you never hear back, it doesn't hurt to try and contact them.

As you start out in comedy, you'll probably also meet lots of other beginning comedians. Don't just think of them as competition or as bad comedians—you're all in the same boat, and you're all struggling to do the same thing, so work together! Ask other beginning comedians what they've found works and doesn't work for them. Find out if there are classes you can take, or other people you should talk to. The people who are learning alongside you can really help you get farther, and you can help them out too.

You can also try contacting established comedians to see if they can give you any advice. They might not have time to answer every e-mail from new comedians, but you might get a response. Every comedian was brand new once, and many of them remember that and are happy to give advice to other comedians.

Text-Dependent Questions

1. What are some ways you can watch other comedians perform? Why should you be watching others?
2. Who can you practice your comedy routines in front of?
3. How can you practice your comedic writing?
4. What is networking, and why is it important?
5. Who can help you get ahead in the comedy world?

Becoming a comedian isn't easy—but as you can see from photographs of celebrities throughout this book, some people do make it. They worked hard at improving their skills, met the right people, and probably stumbled on some luck. If you want to become a comedian, start working at it now. You never know where your skills and hard work will take you!

Find Out More

Online

Connected Comedy
connectedcomedy.com

Famous Comedians
www.biography.com/people/groups/comedians

Humor and Laughter History
www.humor-laughter.com/historyofhumorandlaughter.html

Humor Mall.com
humormall.com

Second City
www.secondcity.com

In Books

Becker, Helaine. *Funny Business: Clowning Around, Practical Jokes, Cool Comedy, Cartooning, and More.* Toronto, Ont.: Maple Tree Press, 2005.

Elliot, Rob. *Laugh-Out-Loud Jokes for Kids.* Grand Rapids, Mich.: Revel, 2010.

Quijano, Jonathan. *Make Your Own Comedy.* North Mankato, Minn.: Capstone Press, 2012.

Schuman, Michael A. *Tina Fey: TV Comedy Superstar.* Berkeley Heights, N.J.: Enslow Publishers, 2011.

Wilshin, Mark. *Cinematic History: Comedy.* North Mankato, Minn.: Heinemann-Raintree, 2005.

Series Glossary of Key Terms

Abstract: Made up of shapes that are symbolic. You might not be able to tell what a piece of abstract art is just by looking at it.

Classical: A certain kind of art traditional to the ancient Greek and Roman civilizations. In music, it refers to music in a European tradition that includes opera and symphony and that is generally considered more serious than other kinds of music.

Culture: All the arts, social meanings, thoughts, and behaviors that are common in a certain country or group.

Gallery: A room or a building that displays art.

Genre: A category of art, all with similar characteristics or styles.

Impressionism: A style of painting that focuses more on the artist's perception of movement and lighting than what something actually looks like.

Improvisation: Created without planning or preparation.

Medium (media): The materials or techniques used to create a work of art. Oil paints are a medium. So is digital photography.

Pitch: How high or low a musical note is; where it falls on a scale.

Portfolio: A collection of some of the art an artist has created, to show off her talents.

Realism: Art that tries to show something exactly as it appears in real life.

Renaissance: A period of rapid artistic and literary development during the 1500s–1700s, or the name of the artistic style from this period.

Studio: A place where an artist can work and create his art.

Style: A certain way of creating art specific to a person or time period.

Technique: A certain way of creating a piece of art.

Tempo: How fast a piece of music goes.

Venue: The location or facility where an event takes place.

Index

About the Author

Z.B. Hill is a an author and publicist living in Binghamton, New York. He has a special interest in education and how art can be used in the classroom.

Picture Credits

Dreamstime.com:
6: Scott Griessel
8: Sbukley
12: Dave Bredeson
14: Carrienelson1
34: Simonwedege
36: Kentannenbaum
38: Kentannenbaum
39: Sean Pavone
40: Kalvis Kalsers
44: Aniram
46: Daniel Raustadt
48: Laurence Agron
50: Artur Marciniec

51: Sean Pavone
52: Laurence Agron
54: Laurence Agron

10: Direct Media, The Yorck Project
20: Giovanni Dall'Orto, Ancient Angora Museum, Athens
22: Musée Carnavalet
18: anastasios71 | Fotolia.com
24: Library of Congress
26: Columbia Pictures Corporation
28: NBC
30: Brooksfilms LTD